D0883891

WITHDRAWN
UTSA LIBRARIES

THE INTERNATIONAL

PROBLEM OF

GOVERNING MANKIND

Volumes in This Series

THE INTERNATIONAL
PROBLEM OF
GOVERNING MANKIND

by

Philip C. Jessup
Columbia University

Foreword by
GEORGE C. S. BENSON

CLAREMONT, CALIFORNIA

1947

COPYRIGHT 1947
CLAREMONT COLLEGE, CLAREMONT, CALIFORNIA

Published by Claremont College
Claremont, California, for
The four Associated Colleges at Claremont
POMONA COLLEGE
SCRIPPS COLLEGE
CLAREMONT MEN'S COLLEGE
CLAREMONT COLLEGE

CONTENTS

FOREWORD

THESE addresses were delivered by Professor Jessup as the eighth in an annual series of lectures conducted by the Associated Colleges in Claremont. Their terse freshness adds much to the thoughts of those who are concerned with world organization. To the man of action, the chance to read through and think over these pages may be worth more than several hundred pages of erudite details.

Professor Jessup does not run around or away from problems, but takes pleasure in considering some of the more difficult ones. He considers carefully but rejects as now impractical the often expressed desire for a world government, based upon an assembly of the peoples, not the governments, of the world. He puts the veto power of the United Nations Security Council in a more favorable light than usual when he points out that it is a very natural holdover from the previously accepted rule of unanimity in international conferences, and that the use elsewhere in the United Nations of majority rule represents a great step forward in international affairs. He considers carefully and rejects the contention that a world organization must guarantee the democracy of its members as do the American and Swiss federations.

Nor does his thought lack up-to-dateness. He does not hesitate to comment directly and critically upon what may be called the method of the Truman Doc-

trine of aid to Greece and Turkey. He deplores the
initial failure of the administration to render such aid
as far as possible through United Nations auspices.
Similarly he digs deeply into the current problems of
the United Nations Secretariat, the organization of
effective international administration, and the presence
of national pressures on men working in the Secretariat.

Professor Jessup's approach is a good balance of long
range idealism with recognition of the importance of
immediate practical problems. He does not reject
world government as an ultimate goal, but he points
very clearly to the difficulties attendant upon immediate accomplishment of it. He has achieved that rare
equilibrium attained only by men who can both think
about and do things. He views the paths to consciousness of an international community of interests as slow
and rocky, but still passable.

Professor Jessup has come to his role of informed
critic on international organization from a wealth of
governmental and academic background. He has
taught international law at Columbia since 1925, and
has distinguished himself among the savants in his
field by serving as one of the editors of the American
Journal of International Law, and writing several
books on technical phases of international law as well
as a noted biography of Elihu Root. His governmental
experience has included service as assistant to Mr. Root
in the Conference of Jurists on the Permanent Court
of International Justice; service in the Office for Foreign Relief in the State Department in 1943; as Assist-
ant-Secretary General of the United Nations Relief
and Rehabilitation and the Bretton Woods confer-

ences, and as technical assistant at the San Francisco Conference.

The Associated Colleges—Pomona College, Scripps College, Claremont Men's College and Claremont College—are happy to make these lectures available to the public. In doing so they wish particularly to express their appreciation to one hundred business and professional leaders of Southern California who have given the necessary financial support as a token of ever increasing interest of the Southwest in problems of public policy.

GEORGE C. S. BENSON.

THE INTERNATIONAL

PROBLEM OF

GOVERNING MANKIND

I

A LOOK BEFORE A LEAP INTO
WORLD GOVERNMENT

WORLD government has long been an ideal. It has recently become a program of action. The program is supported by persons of widely differing interests and temperaments. Its sponsorship is no longer confined to idealistic theorists and the "lunatic fringe." Judges, lawyers, bankers, businessmen, administrators, churchmen, scholars, and plain citizens unite in asserting that world government is not only desirable but also attainable. I shall endeavor to suggest some of the factors which need to be considered by persons of good will who are, in this political sense, agnostics.

The impulse to establish world government is to be attributed to the insistent human yearning for peace. Fresh experience of war is requisite to provide the drive for active campaigns to check this greatest of all human ills. As each modern war has ended, people have insisted that there must not be another and for a time they have struggled to solve the problem. As the memory of the horror fades with the passage of time, the impulse is blunted, the activity decreases. Differences of opinion on details of program split the ranks and enlistments fall off. We have compulsory service to wage war but not to wage peace. Milton declared that,
> "Peace hath her victories
> No less renowned than war,"

but as Elihu Root once remarked, we do not "understand how to make the heroes of peace gorgeous and striking to the imagination."

The theme of many advocates of world government is that war can be abolished only by the elimination of sovereignty. By "sovereignty" they mean the ultimate freedom of national states to enforce their wills by the use of their power. I agree that national sovereignty is the root of the evil. The question of procedure remains. Can the root be pulled up by one mighty revolutionary heave, or should it first be loosened by digging around it and cutting the rootlets one by one? The first procedure requires a stupendous mobilization of labor, carefully coordinated. The second procedure enables a number of parallel efforts to continue simultaneously. The first procedure is that advocated by those who urge world government "now." The second procedure is used by those who would strengthen the United Nations as the symbol of recorded human progress toward the ideal. Professor Robert MacIver, in his recent book "The Web of Government," effectively argues the necessity for the elimination of sovereignty and the defects of the organizational forms of the United Nations with the provisions for the veto of the great states permanently represented in the Security Council. But elsewhere in his book he notes that "a strong argument can be made for the case that great institutional transformations more frequently result from step-by-step modifications than from the spasmodic upheavals of once-for-all revolutions."

Objection will be taken to the assertion that "world government now" implies revolutionary action. I do not suggest that the advocates of this plan are plotting the forcible overthrow of existing governments. Indeed it is one of the weaknesses of their position that they assume the possibility of adopting immediately a world constitution at some great town meeting of the world. In the most pungent analysis of the world government arguments which has appeared, Nathan Pelcovits has well pointed out that "Constitution-making is the final step in establishing a regime of law and order."[1] Unless there is a preëxisting community in the real sense of that term, the adoption of a constitution may, like revolution, in MacIver's words, "do more to demonstrate the preëxisting lack of harmony than to substitute a new harmony."

We are faced with a problem of enormous scope and complexity. Inside national states we are in a stage of rapidly growing interference by government in the affairs of the individual. The movement has gone much further in other countries than in the United States. In this country the history of the movement, from the opposition to the establishment of such bodies as the Interstate Commerce Commission and the Federal Trade Commission which are now taken so much for granted, down to the present year, may be pictured on a graph with sharp ups and downs. Each progression is followed by a recession but the general curve of the graph shows an upward trend in terms of increased state controls. We appear today to be in a period of check or recession. In the international field there is equally a fairly steady upward curve registering the increasing restrictions placed upon the unfettered action of sovereign states. Where the restrictions have been imposed, as upon conquered states after a war,

---

[1] Harpers Magazine, November, 1946, p. 396.

there has been a sharp rebound as soon as political conditions made that possible. Where the restrictions have been assumed in treaties freely negotiated, they have also been subject to political depressions as is illustrated by the history of the League of Nations in the late 1930's. Internationally, we are now in a period of progression, with limitations on sovereignty, already assumed through the United Nations Charter and contemplated in various current official proposals far more extensive than anything which the past has called into being.

In the national field, shifts in the trend toward more or less governmental· control are usually the consequence of a change of the political party in power, brought about by peaceful balloting. In the international field the shifts are usually the result of war. One of the great problems of international politics today is that of finding a method of peaceful progress in the direction of greater international control. It must not come so fast as to provoke resistance, which is war; it cannot come so slowly as to leave any future aggressor or revolter against oppression eager and free to provoke war again. The danger of war is so terrible and so acute in this atom-splitting age that we are forced to take the risk of too much rather than too little international control of sovereignty. One must also realize that the requisite restrictions on sovereignty are not confined to limiting the use of force, the banning of atomic bombs and the outlawry of war itself. Restrictions such as those are necessary particularly to guard against a recurrence of situations in which some fanatical leader seeks to secure for himself or his country the domination of the world. Other restrictions on sovereignty are necessary to meet the legitimate aspirations of peoples who have never attained a reasonably good life. These restrictions involve the control of the old freedom to wage selfish and monopolistic economic war through high tariffs, cartels, colonial exploitation, or any other of the familiar devices of imperialism and of economic nationalism. If these social and economic evils are not remedied, desperate peoples will break any pledged word and risk any sanction in the search for a better life.

The existence of government does not mean the end of war as the continuing history of civil war clearly reveals. The argument in Emery Reeves' brilliant little book "The Anatomy of Peace" is riddled by his failure to consider the problem of civil war. It may indeed be true that civil war inside an established world community would be better than war among sovereign states because the outcome of the civil war would be the strengthening of world government. But such a civil war, like international war, would be evidence of the failure of mankind to provide viable institutions and processes for peaceful change of unjust conditions.

There is one important contrast between the dangers which attend the extension of government controls within states and their extension among states in the international society. The complexities of human affairs in both the national and international fields require governmental regulation. Governmental controls are necessary whenever and wherever human nature pursues a selfish end to the injury of the weaker members of society. In the national field the danger is that as governmental controls increase, the freedom of the individual decreases until government becomes the master instead of the servant of the people. As we progress in international organization, we are laying increasing stress upon the individual. The numerous references to fundamental human rights and freedoms in the Charter of the United Nations bear witness to that fact. In other words, international controls are being invoked to redress the balance between the national government and the individual in order that the individual may have a more perfect freedom. But international controls thereby restrict the sovereignty of states, who for this purpose may be likened to the constituents or to the "individuals" in the world society. Because sovereignty has been the chief obstacle in the way of the elimination of war, this result of international controls is welcome. It will be welcome until world organization or world government develops to a point at which the human being himself is again too greatly checked and throttled by the bureaucratic weight of government. Again it may be said that at this present stage the immediate dangers are so great that we must take the risk of too much rather than too little government on the international scale. When we have mastered the problem of war we shall be free to devote ourselves more effectively to the still more basic problem of guarding "the dignity and worth of the human person," as that phrase is used in the preamble of the United Nations Charter.

Let us turn to the difficulties of international governmental organization.

Perhaps the first as well as the last problem to be faced is the method by which agreement upon further improvements in world organization or government is to be achieved. There are those who maintain that more imagination and more courage would have produced at San Francisco two years ago a more perfect instrument.

I do not agree with that view when it is advanced to prove that it would have been possible then to create a world organization with an effective enforcement power uncontrolled by the crippling veto right. It would perhaps have been possible to create an organization to which some states would belong, but there would have existed beside it another group of states in another organization. The result would have been the creation of two separate alliances and we should have been forced to create another super-organization to regulate conflicts between the two camps. In that super-organization, I maintain the veto would have reappeared. All proposals for international organization which contemplate a partial membership with strong states outside are subject to the same fundamental objection. They are misleading and dangerous. It is a weakness of the United Nations that its Charter did not go further and adopt the principle of universality of membership. It would have been far wiser statesmanship to have compelled the enemy states like Germany and Japan to accept the Charter at once, than to leave them outside of it. There is no reason to despair that such universality will not be attained within a reasonable time by the United Nations under its present Charter.

If it be true that the San Francisco conferees could not have established a general international organization governed by majority rule even in matters of ultimate enforcement of the peace, then there is no reason to believe that another conference convened today would achieve different results in this respect. It is true that in the past two years we have seen important indications that even some of the great powers are ready for further restrictions on their liberty of action. There have been official statements to that effect in Great Britain. The United States' proposals for the controls to be exercised by an international atomic energy authority mark a notable advance. The new French constitution asserts that "on the basis of reciprocity, France agrees to limitations on its sovereignty necessary for the organization and defense of peace." No similar suggestion has come from Moscow, and Russia is an indispensable partner in any such enterprise for the reason already stated. We are making progress but we are making it partly because the first steps were taken at San Francisco.

It is argued that different results would be secured if there were a conference of the peoples of the world instead of a conference of their governments. This is wishful thinking. It stems from the glib assumption that the world is already democratic. It is not even true, as some allege, that the world outside of Russia is democratic. There are some six dozen states in the world; in a very large number of them the mass of the people are not politically literate. In much of Latin America, the Middle East, and Asia, people would not know what you were talking about if you said they are members of "one world." In many of those countries and in Russia, the suggestion that there could be free popular elections of delegates to a world assembly and that those delegates would represent the people and not the governments, is fantastic. Even in countries far more advanced in democratic government, it has been found necessary in the past to provide for international supervision of plebiscites to enable the people to express their will on an immediate local issue which could be presented in broad terms and not in the form of the election of an individual representative. It is no simple matter to organize international supervision of elections in all the countries of the world in which such a process would be needed to attain the desired result. One has only to consider the fact that we do not now have a world government which could compel states to submit to that kind of supervision which they would—quite properly—take to be a reflection upon their local administration. Even if the international supervision could be provided, it is inconceivable that persons who were not merely representative of the national government and who were yet sufficiently wise and well-informed to aid in the drafting of a world constitution, could be nominated and elected by popular referendum. Consider the difficulty even in these United States of running for national office without the support of an established political party.

It is impossible to escape the conclusion that a world constitution or new plan of international organization can be achieved only through the action of governments and their representatives.

In elaborating the actual form of international organization it will be necessary to face a perennial problem of all government, which is the reconciliation of the needs of centralization and of decentralization. In the growing structure of the United Nations, the tendency is to create separate organizations to handle separate problems. Thus we already have organizations dealing with health, civil aviation, labor, food and agriculture, relief, education, science and culture, transportation, and a variety of other topics. The Charter foresaw this development and provided for the integration of these various specialized agencies within the overall framework of the United Nations Organization. The Economic and Social Council is the organ of the United Nations to which the task of unification of effort is entrusted. It is still undecided whether a rather rigid form of control will be exercised through supervision of the budgets of the various specialized agencies. There is a natural tendency on the part of each agency to develop its own personality and *esprit de corps*. Particularly, well-established bodies such as the International Labor Organization, tend to struggle for the maintenance of the greatest possible autonomy. Because of the size and complexity of the world problems with which these various organizations must deal, it is highly desirable that the work be decentralized. At the same time it is essential that effort and funds be conserved by some arrangement for the avoidance of duplication and conflict. These are not problems which can be disposed of once and for all by some magic administrative formula. The solutions must be found step by step as the work progresses.

At the last meeting of the General Assembly the same outcry which is heard in Washington, was raised against the development of an international bureaucracy. The budget estimates of the Secretary General were reduced and an increased load of work is being carried by a diminished staff. It is probably true that under the urgent pressure of setting up an organization which had to begin functioning immediately, there was the usual amount of overstaffing in the administrative divisions of the Secretariat. Americans, with their highly developed theories and techniques of public administration, are particularly prone to build up an elaborate administrative machine functioning under a multitude of rules and regulations designed to grind out answers as automatically as one of the great calculators developed by the International Business Machines Corporation. The result of this process in any governmental unit is the creation of red tape. The length of the red tape measures the extent of the human mind's incapacity to deal with a complex problem. It is probably inevitable that a certain number of matters in any large administrative unit should be handled according to an automatic rule instead of on the basis of a consideration of the individual merits of a particular case. When, however, the clientele of the administrative unit is composed of sovereign states and their official representatives, the elements of prestige and of wounded feelings are just as important as the requirement of efficiency in the discharge of a task. For example, in the personnel section of the United Nations Secretariat, it may be possible to deal in a routine way with the thousands of individual applications for jobs. It is impossible to deal in a routine way with communications from governments concerning matters which may seem small in themselves but to which the government may attach very great importance.

An international organization must also struggle with the difficulties created by the fact that in drawing its officials from more than 50 different countries, it draws into itself dozens of different concepts of proper methods of administration. The point may be illustrated by the analogous situation in regard to the rules of parliamentary procedure. At international conferences it has long been true that serious friction arises from different parliamentary practices. For instance, in many countries the rather rigid formality of the rules obtaining in the United States and England concerning the making of motions and the necessity of having a motion seconded, are unfamiliar. The projection of this problem is found in the whole question of distinguishing procedural and substantive issues. Since the question of the veto and of the requisite majority in the organs of the United Nations frequently depends on whether a question is or is not procedural, this difficulty is crucial.

Another problem which confronts both the government of the United States and the United Nations Organization is that of delegation of power to the constituent governmental units. In the United States, the federal government has acted in a variety of matters which had earlier been left to the several states because the latter failed to deal adequately with problems which attracted general interest. In the international picture the various states have an even stronger feeling about their sovereignty and the desirability of maintaining their freedom in regulating their internal affairs. This concern is reflected in the provision in Article 2 of the Charter which prohibits the United Nations from intervening "in matters which are essentially within the domestic jurisdiction of any state." The only exception is in cases where the international community needs to take common action to prevent a breach of the peace. The realm of "domestic questions" is not clearly defined. It was recognized at the San Francisco Conference that any question, in these interdependent days, make take on an international aspect. It has already become clear that the general provisions in the Charter concerning respect for fundamental human rights may justify the organized international community in taking steps to prevent any state from abusing its own nationals, although a state's treatment of its own citizens used to be considered an entirely domestic question. The controversy between India and the Union of South Africa at the last meeting of the General Assembly was illustrative of this point. The new peace treaties impose obligations on the former enemy states to safeguard fundamental human rights and freedoms; such treaties would clearly provide a basis for action by the United Nations in case of a denial of those rights in those countries. Just as in this country, movements such as those for the regulation of child labor led to federal action to overcome the slothfulness of the individual states, so the welling demands for an international bill of rights and its implementation will eventually lead to action by the international organization, unless the states of the world put their own houses in order. Similarly in the economic field, federal regulation in the United States has been necessary to safeguard the economic interests of the whole country. In the international field, the failure of the several states to regulate and control unfair international trade practices is leading to an international agreement to establish the International Trade Organization. At this rudimentary stage of international organization such treaties are the nearest equivalent to international legislation.

The answer to grumblings about the danger of establishing an international bureaucracy is to be found
in the improvement of local conditions and the practices and policies of the states of the world. If the
states are prepared to adopt policies which will remedy
acknowledged ills, the international organization can
delegate control of these matters to the states. This
process has worked effectively in the control of such
evils as the illicit international traffic in narcotics. It
remains to be seen how far international action will be
required to supplant or to supervise national action in
other fields.

THE PROBLEM OF STAFFING

No matter how perfect the Charter or Constitution
under which a frame of international or national government is created, administration will not succeed
unless it is in the hands of the proper personnel. The
League of Nations succeeded in creating a body of
international civil servants with a remarkable amount
of devotion to the international service. The credit for
the League's achievement in this field is largely due to
the courage with which Sir Eric Drummond, the first
Secretary-General, attacked the problem of selecting
his staff. Mr. Trygve Lie has shown great courage and
independence in the discharge of many of his functions
as Secretary-General of the United Nations. According to Article 101 of the Charter, "the paramount consideration in the employment of the staff and in the
determination of the conditions of service shall be the
necessity of securing the highest standards of efficiency, competence, and integrity. Due regard shall be
paid to the importance of recruiting the staff on as

wide a geographical basis as possible." The principle
of broad geographical representation is a sound one for
an international organization. Inevitably there will be
cases where particular positions will need to be filled
by persons coming from certain countries or areas
which are inadequately represented in the Secretariat.
This is bound to mean that in some cases the best available candidate will not get the job. The danger is that
even within the principle of geographical distribution,
the Secretary-General will not be free to select the
person of his choice, but that he will need to consider
the individual's acceptability to his own government.
It is deplorable that at the very outset the United States
did not take a firm and consistent position which might
have set a precedent for non-interference in appointments to the Secrtariat and which might also have established the precedent that the service of the United
Nations is so important that even a most valuable of-
ficer of a national government should be released for
that broader service. One qualification must be noted.
In regard to appointments of the highest officials in
the Secretariat of the United Nations attention must
be paid to the fact that these persons represent contact
points with some of the most influential members of
the Organization. If such officials are not personally
acceptable to their own governments they cannot
successfully carry out their liaison functions.

Nevertheless, every member of the Secretariat is required to subscribe to an oath or declaration "to exercise in all loyalty, discretion, and conscience the
functions entrusted to me as a member of the international service of the United Nations, to discharge
those functions and regulate my conduct with the

interests of the United Nations only in view and not to seek or accept instructions in regard to the performance of my duties from any government or other authority external to the Organization." By Article 100 of the Charter, the member states promise "to respect the exclusively international character of the responsibilities of the Secretary-General and the staff and not to seek to influence them in the discharge of their responsibilities."

Demands for political and geographical representation are not peculiar to international organizations. It may be well to recall the fact that up to forty years ago it was customary in the United States to allot not only top diplomatic posts but in general all diplomatic and consular offices to the various states on the demand of their senators and congressmen. The situation was even worse when a state had no representative belonging to the political party in power. Secretary of State Root once recalled a conversation with Senator Spooner. The senator called at Root's office in the State Department shortly after the latter's appointment and said "The consulate at . . . is open and that belongs to me, and I'll give you a man for it." "The devil you will!" said Root. He told the senator his state would have its share of appointments and when those appointments were to be made he would consult the senator about them; if he put up good men, his recommendations would be regarded. Another senator called on Root very early one morning at the State Department with a similar demand only to be told by the Secretary of State: "Senator, you ought not to take a drink every morning before breakfast—it isn't good for you. And you ought not to get a consulate every morning before breakfast—that isn't good for you."

The laws governing our foreign service have been much improved, both in terms of the selection of candidates and in terms of their compensation and opportunities for advancement, but there is still plenty of room for improvement. Proposals for legislation creating a "West Point" or "Annapolis" for diplomats are supported by glib arguments about democracy in the foreign service but actually would tend to throw our diplomatic career back into the clutches of the spoilsman. Again, congressmen who wish to obtain credit for reducing taxes or building local bridges or mending political fences are apt to think that slashes in our international budget will arouse the least opposition among their constituents. It is the responsibility of the individual taxpayer and voter to register his conviction that it is false economy to cripple the government agency which has the responsibility for maintaining international peace. Contrasted with the average citizen of Great Britain, for example, we are soft and self-indulgent in trying to avoid the inevitable cost of the aftermath of war and of the responsibilities of our world position. I agree that one of our principal contributions must consist of a demonstration that our system of life works. I do not agree that such demonstration requires us to have two lumps of sugar in every cup of coffee and a candy-bar in every mouth when millions are starving in other lands. We do not add to our stature as world leaders merely by adding to our individual waistlines.

The international civil service is protected by provisions requiring states to extend to its members such immunities as are necessary to enable them to discharge their functions. In the general convention or treaty prepared by the General Assembly of the United Nations relative to these privileges and immunities, it is explained that they are accorded to the representatives of Members and to officials of the Secretariat "not for the personal benefit of the individuals themselves" but "in the interests of the United Nations" and "in order to safeguard the independent exercise of their functions in connection with the United Nations."

The United States has made progress in providing the required immunities except in the matter of taxation. The Treasury Department still takes the provincial view that American citizens serving on an international secretariat should not enjoy the immunities from income taxes on their salaries which alien members of the Secretariat enjoy. They insist on asserting that the granting of immunity would constitute a special favor to one group of American citizens. Actually the United States by this attitude is merely taking money out of its own pocket and the pockets of other members of the United Nations. American citizens on the Secretariat receive a supplement to their base salaries to equalize the amount they are forced to pay in taxes. If that were not done, they would be paid less than their colleagues who receive tax exemption. Our income tax collection in these cases therefore is a tax upon the international organization and its budget. The amount involved is not large but the principle is important. We are years behind other governments in international sophistication because during the interwar period we cut ourselves off from membership in the League of Nations and thus deprived ourselves of the experience in international organizations which the other states obtained.

Congress became educated only relatively recently to appreciate the importance of our own foreign service; we still show signs of immaturity in handling the affairs of international organizations. When representatives of the United Nations first began coming on official missions to this country, our customs and immigration officials were not adequately instructed concerning their reception and shocking cases of neglect and discourtesy resulted. Now that the world capital is located in the United States we must be more adequately prepared to play the role of host in accordance with the customs and necessities of international intercourse. Recently a judge of the City Court of New Rochelle, New York, was called upon to rule upon the immunities of the chauffeur of the Secretary-General of the United Nations. Pending Senate approval of a United Nations treaty defining such immunities, the subject is covered by very general language in the Charter, and in an act of Congress. The Charter itself is, of course, a treaty and under the Constitution is part of the supreme law of the land. But the Charter is a constitutional document which lays down broad principles rather than detailed rules. The judge in denying immunity from arrest in this case was obviously unfamiliar with two centuries of law and practice relative to the comparable problem of immunities for the diplomatic representatives of foreign states and could see no reason why the immunities for the United Nations staff should differ from those accorded members of state and federal legislatures. Without going into more detail, the case is cited as evidence of the need in this enlightened country for more understanding of the nature of international organization and the responsibilities of the United States as the host country.

In one other respect we still, as a nation, have not displayed the amount of wisdom which it is to be hoped we shall soon acquire. We still seem to have the idea that in the selection of members of our delegations to meetings of the General Assembly, it is more important to have an eye on our own Congress than on the important negotiations with which these delegates are entrusted. It is an excellent principle to draw members of the Senate and House into active participation in international affairs with which so many of them are woefully unfamiliar. But the interests of the United States in so vital a matter as the preservation of the peace of the world cannot be handled as a sideshow of domestic politics. We need as delegates persons who are familiar with the business at hand, who are prepared to devote themselves to it and to utilize the staffs of technical advisers which the State Department places at their disposal. Some of our delegates have been highly competent people; some have not. Much of the work of the United Nations is of a continuing character and we shall need to utilize the full-time services of trained men and women as we do in our representation in the embassies and legations accredited to individual foreign countries. The fact that we still do not provide adequate compensation and allowances to permit any but persons of independent wealth to accept appointments to our top diplomatic posts is a disgrace—not a precedent to be followed with regard to the United Nations.

A further problem which arises in connection with international organization involves the scheduling and the conduct of meetings. If one goes back 100 years in the history of diplomacy, one finds that when an international conference was held it was distinctly a meeting of separate states which had no thought of merging their individuality in the group. Gradually, as the conference habit became more fully developed, one sees the emergence of the notion that the conference or group has a personality of its own. Certain decisions are made by the group as such and not solely by an exercise of the combined wills of the individual participants. Out of this development we begin to get the practice of majority rule in international affairs. At first majority decisions are accepted only in minor procedural matters. As the international community began to regulate the technical aspects of its relationships through organizations known as "public international unions," such questions as the international regulation of posts, telegraph, cables, radio, and other activities especially in the fields of transportation and communication, are left to the management of permanent staffs and to majority decisions in meetings either of groups equivalent to executive committees or of all the members.

When the League of Nations system developed, the states were not yet ready to accept the principle of majority rule in important political questions. The League Council and Assembly therefore still operated in general upon the principle of unanimity. Thus the single vote of a small state like Persia was able to prevent the adoption of a proposal to which all other members of the League agreed. On procedural questions, majority decisions were accepted, but serious disagreements arose relative to defining the distinction between procedural and substantive matters.

Some of the difficulties were avoided by the use of

the committee system. It became usual for committees
to reach decisions by majority vote. This practice had
developed in earlier international conferences and was
utilized even more effectively at Geneva. The reason
why this deviation from the principle of unanimity
was acceptable is obvious; commiteee reports were
generally merely recommendations to the Council or
Assembly and states had an opportunity in those larger
bodies to approve or to reject the recommendations of
the committee. But recommendations of committees
frequently were so inherently persuasive that it became much more difficult for a single state to oppose a
recommendation which came before the large body
in this form. Moreover, as a part of the general tech-
nique of diplomatic negotiation in international conferences, it proved to be much easier to iron out the
differences of opinion in small committee meetings and
in informal discussion between committee meetings,
than it was when the representative of a state had to
take a formal position of opposition or support when
a proposition was first presented in a plenary meeting.
Examples of the successful use of this committee procedure could be drawn not only from the experience
of the League of Nations, but also from that of the
Pan-American conferences and of numerous other
international gatherings.

Still another development has taken place as a result
of the emergence of the idea that the conference or the
organization itself is an international personality which
speaks with authority. In the older practice, it was
customary for the conference to agree upon the text
of a treaty which was then submitted to the states for
ratification. As the experience of the League demon-

strated, even where there was no strong opposition to the treaty, indifference or inertia frequently delayed or prevented such ratifications. In most states the department of state or foreign office would have to submit the treaty to a legislative body for approval. It is not necessary to look beyond the borders of the United States to recall the difficulty of securing prompt action on treaties in legislative halls. An interesting attempt to grapple with this problem was made by the Constitution of the International Labor Organization. Under that Constitution the members of the Organization assumed the obligation to submit all treaties adopted at one of the conferences to the appropriate national authorities with a view to securing appropriate action. Another device has been found particularly useful in the inter-American conferences. Instead of agreeing upon a formal treaty which was subject to ratification, the conference would adopt a resolution expressing a general view upon some problem under consideration. Thus at the Lima Conference of 1938 there was unanimous adoption of a statement to the effect that it had become part of the public law of the Americas that the acquisition of territory by forceful conquest was illegal.

The United Nations is building upon the accumulation of these international experiences. The question of the veto in the Security Council has been generally presented in a false light. Many people have started from the assumption that majority rule is the standard and that the veto power represents a retreat from that standard. Actually, in international affairs, the unanimity rule was the standard and the adoption of the principle of majority vote in all cases except those in which the veto applies, was a distinct advance from the traditional position. In the General Assembly, the Charter does not require a unanimous vote in any case, although in certain important matters a two-thirds majority is specified. In the Economic and Social Council and in the Trusteeship Council the majority rule prevails. In the Security Council, much of the important business is carried on without involving the right of veto, which is to say that majority rule governs in many instances. It is true that in the most important cases the right of veto does apply. This is a very serious defect in the development of international machinery for the preservation of international peace. But the surprising thing is not that the great powers have retained their traditional right to prevent common agreements by a negative vote; the surprising thing is that all but five states in the world have relinquished the principle of unanimity and have accepted majority rule. The importance of this progress cannot be exaggerated. It is also notable that even among the great powers there have been modifications of attitudes since the United States proposed the veto formula at Yalta and since the Charter was adopted at San Francisco. The United States as well as the Soviet Union still insist that the right of veto must be retained in respect of the application of sanctions in case of a breach of the peace. But the United States advocates the relinquishment of the veto in crucial matters connected with the control of the new atomic weapons. It is familiar ground that on this point the Soviet Union still remains adamant in its support of the veto.

One other development merits mention in this connection. One sees in the work of the United Nations the further development of a practice which was not unknown at Geneva, namely, the practice of abstaining from voting. In cases where a state is not in favor of a proposition or, where for domestic reasons it does not wish to be recorded as favoring a proposal, but where its opposition is not deep and strong, its representative may abstain from voting so that the necessary majority or unanimity is obtained.

The development of democratic processes or majority rule in international meetings has very definitely improved the position of the small states. The spokesmen of the small states found at Geneva, and find in the United Nations, a forum in which their voices may be heard and may be carried throughout the world. This is no negligible progress from the days when the Concert of Europe acted on behalf of the civilized world. Moreover, the small states have not been slow to learn that when a majority vote is required, it is possible for a group of small states to secure important concessions by presenting a united front. As a result, we have seen examples of bloc voting with the Latin American group and the Arab League presenting the more notable examples.

Is there any reason to believe that the substitution of world government for the United Nations would overcome the problem of the veto? It would do so only on the assumption that if a world government were established, the delegates in the organs of that government would all rid themselves of the present insistence upon the ultimate control of matters which they consider vital to their safety. If that change of heart has taken or does take place on a world-wide scale, the particular difficulty of the veto could as well be eliminated through the unanimous adoption of an amendment to the Charter as through the formation of a world government. The difficulty again is that many advocates of world government proceed upon the fallacious view that even in the present state of the world it is possible to register the voice of the people without going through the channels of the governments of the several states.

In considering this specific question of voting in international gatherings, I am not overlooking the fact that further evolution in the understanding of the mutual advantage which all peoples would derive from a subordination of individual free will to the common good and to the common decision, would mark a tremendous progress along the road toward the elimination of war. I would repeat, however, that in dealing with a unit so large as is the world, it is impossible to manage the affairs of the peoples of the world without very considerable delegation of power to local units of government or administration.

This problem of sheer size introduces a further difficulty into the operation of an international assemblage. Whether one has a world assembly composed of representatives of states (as in the Senate of the United States) or composed of representatives chosen by some such criterion as the size of population (as in our House of Representatives) a large and somewhat unwieldy body results. Considerable thought was devoted to the question of the maximum size of delegations in the General Assembly of the United Nations. The Charter provides that each member of the United Nations is entitled to five delegates, but each delegation casts only one vote.

Whenever the General Assembly meets, it finds upon its agenda a great variety of problems, some of which are political, some economic, some social, some legal, and some purely administrative or budgetary. Any such body must do its work through committees which undertake the preliminary exploration of the topic under consideration. In order to get through its business, these various committees must meet simultaneously. It is at this point that the small states find themselves at a distinct disadvantage since they frequently cannot afford to send the full quota of delegates supported by the necessary experts and interpreters to enable them to take an active part in the work of all these committees. The congressional delegation of the State of California is not composed of persons selected with a view to giving the state in the House of Representatives one expert on labor, another on taxation, another on agriculture, another on commerce, another on international affairs, and so on. Every congressman is an expert on every subject and thus may serve on any committee when seniority rights bring him his turn. National states, in choosing delegations to international conferences, generally seek to include experts on the topics which will be on the agenda. In the House of Representatives in Washington, we have gotten away from the idea that every state has an individual interest which requires representation on every one of the committees of the House. The same is true of the Senate. In the international field it is still true that most states are not ready to entrust the representation of their interests to representatives whom they have not chosen. There are instances in which some Latin American states have been

content to have their particular point of view represented by other Latin American states, and to a certain
extent this principle operates among the members of
the British Commonwealth of Nations. But even in
Washington we find that sectional interests are frequently important. Only through the gradual and
frequently disappointingly slow process of the development of a consciousness of international community interests, will the delegates coming from various parts of the world feel free of the necessity of
representing the particular needs and desires of their
own area and group, even though that group relin-
quishes some aspects of its sovereignty in the acceptance of more highly developed forms of world government.

When it comes to action, an international organization can operate in a variety of ways. It is only in the
extreme case that it becomes necessary to marshall the
combined armed forces of the international community to suppress the law breakers.

International organizations, even in their present
primitive form, can exercise important and perhaps
decisive influence in many situations which, if left to
themselves, might bring about general war. As already
suggested, the simple airing of a controversy in the
world forum has its value. The passing of a resolution,
even though it has no binding force, may be influential. This would seem to be true of the General Assembly's resolution concerning India's complaint
against South Africa about the mistreatment of Indians
in the latter country. Despite the South African view
that this whole question was outside the competence
of the General Assembly, reports indicate that the

General Assembly's resolution has been influential in inducing the South African government to take steps to ameliorate the position of the Indians among its population.

The organization may take the next step of appointing a commission to investigate and report. Thus the complex situation in Greece resulted in the appointment of a United Nations commission which is conducting investigations on the spot. Fifty years ago, if a state like Albania had fired on a British warship and brought about the sinking of two destroyers with considerable loss of life, Great Britain would undoubtedly have used its own power to secure satisfaction. At present Great Britain has brought the case before the Security Council which appointed a small committee to report on the facts and on the applicable rules of law.

It is disappointing to one primarily interested in the development of international law and international judicial processes to note that in neither the South African case nor the Albanian case did the organs of the United Nations choose to refer the legal issues to the International Court of Justice for an advisory opinion. The League of Nations found this procedure an extremely useful one, and there was no instance in which the opinion of the old World Court was flouted. But in the early days of the League, when Italy bombarded and occupied the Greek island of Corfu in order to secure satisfaction for the assassination of the Italian member of a boundary commission, the League referred the matter to a special commission which brought in an evasive report. The old World Court came into being in September, 1921. Its first business came in May, 1922, when the Council of the League of Nations made its first request for an advisory opinion. The first contested case came before the Court for judgment in January, 1923. The Supreme Court of the United States came into being on February 1, 1790; during the first three years of its existence it had practically no business to transact.[2] It is much too soon to despair of the development of law and justice through the United Nations.

In many situations any international organization or government will have to operate through local governmental machinery, whether that machinery be embodied in sovereign states or in political subdivisions of a genuine world community. In the United States law enforcement is to a very large extent the function of the local or state governments and not the function of the federal government. It is only when the disturbance attains such dimensions as to exceed the competence of the local group that federal forces are employed. The same thing is true in regard to international affairs whether one is dealing with such matters as the regulation of the international traffic in narcotics, with the production of atomic energy, or with the basic problem of the prevention of war. As our own experience with labor troubles indicates, there are bound to be situations in which competing interests in the community are sufficiently strong and well balanced to make it impossible to impose governmental decision by force. With all of our highly developed governmental processes and national unity, we have not been ready to impose general compulsory

[2] Charles Warren, The Supreme Court in United States History (1924), Vol. I., p. 57.

processes for the settlement of labor disputes. Is it then surprising that the far less cohesive world community has failed to reach that stage in the adjustment of disputes between different groups and peoples?

The idea of international solidarity and of a world community is growing. I see no evidence that it has yet grown to the point which would make possible the adoption and operation of a world constitution which, as pointed out earlier, is the final and not the preliminary stage in the development of a political community. Some who share this view concerning the impracticability of world government at this time definitely oppose the agitation for world government. I do not share this latter view. As John Stuart Mill effectively argued, there is value in general discussion of all proposals in order that people may develop their thinking and formulate their own conclusions. The view of some adherents of world government that any support for the United Nations is treason to the cause of progression toward the development of a real world community, seems to me as unreasonable as that of the supporters of the United Nations who are unwilling to listen to arguments for world government now. It is encouraging to note that the recent program adopted by a group of organizations advocating world government takes a much more tolerant position and inclines much more to the evolutionary principle.

Charles Morgan in his "Reflections in a Mirror" suggests some views which Metternich might express today if he were discussing the current scene. This is what he imagines Metternich might say:

"A peace that ends a great war should be regarded neither as a sleeping draught nor as a stimulant.

Peace is like a pair of stockings. My life consisted
in darning Europe's stockings. But you are too lazy.
Remember what Goethe said to Eckerman: 'Man is
not born to solve the problems of the Universe but
to find out where the problem lies and then to keep
within the limits of what he can comprehend.' I
would urge you, if you are in pursuit of an ideal, to
take with you a map and a darning-needle."

Plans for a world government are a map, and perhaps
a compass. The United Nations is the darning-needle.

II

INTERNATIONAL GUARANTY OF
DEMOCRATIC GOVERNMENT

THIS paper is written during country-wide debates
concerning a proposed American guaranty of
"democratic" government in two particular states,
Greece and Turkey. The Greek and Turkish problems are not newcomers to the international stage. This
is not the first case of the kind nor the last. The international problem was not created by President Truman's message of March 12, 1947. The problem will
not cease to exist when Greece and Turkey live pros-
perously under governments as democratic and as free
from foreign dangers as is the government of California today. The immediate issue is therefore but a
sample of a continuing problem of international law
and politics; it will be considered here in the broad
frame of the experience of the modern international
society and of the United States as a federal union.

The Constitution of the United States provides, in
Article IV, Section 4, that "The United States shall
guarantee to every State in this Union a Republican
Form of Government, and shall protect each of them
against invasion."

If two factions are contending for the mastery in
one of our states, each maintaining that it is *the* government of the state, what happens? We have recently
been witnessing such a conflict in the State of Georgia;
the Supreme Court of that state decided in favor of one
contestant and the other promptly yielded to the judi-

cial pronouncement. The case affords a happy example of the successful functioning of a "republican form of government" settling a vital dispute in the political unit in which it arose. In earlier times in our history there were more bloody conflicts, less easily solved.

In 1849 the Supreme Court of the United States was called upon to consider the constitutional provision which has been quoted, in a case which arose in Rhode Island. Rhode Island, unlike the other original states of the Union, did not adopt a new constitution at the time of the Revolution but continued to operate under the form of government established by the Charter of Charles the Second, with some few changes. By 1841, many of the citizens of that state had decided that a new constitution was needed. They formed organizations, held meetings and finally convened a constitutional convention which adopted a new constitution. Elections were held and a new governor and other state officers were elected. All of this took place extra-legally without the support or approval of the established government. The governor who was already in office proclaimed martial law and sought to round up the leaders of the opposing party. Armed clashes of troops occurred and the old established government emerged victorious. A leader of the oppostion, appropriately named Martin Luther, was arrested by the militia and sued the arresting officers for trespass; the case was eventually taken to the Supreme Court of the United States. By the time the wheels of justice had ground the preliminaries, Rhode Island had adopted another new constitution by the approved legal methods and peace reigned, but the Supreme Court made a pronouncement on the issues before it. The Court

The historic story of "bleeding Kansas" need not be continued here in detail. It was not long after these events that the Civil War broke out. It broke out in these United States operating with a homogeneous population under a constitution which was the admiration of mankind. The Union before and since faced the problem of rival political factions contending for the mastery. The United Nations under its Charter which seeks to unite peoples which are far from homogeneous, faces like problems today. Has mankind, have the American people, in the intervening decades, learned enough political wisdom to settle such controversies without war?

The Charter of the United Nations contains no such guaranty of a republican form of government as is found in the Constitution of the United States. It could not have done so. In the United States when the Constitution was adopted, the existing governments of the recently liberated colonies were mutually satisfactory one to the other. In the United Nations when the Charter was drafted at San Francisco in 1945, there was no parallel satisfaction. If the Charter had referred to the "democratic" governments of its members, the word would have had very different meanings in at least two of the member states. Russians speak of "democracy" as meaning economic democracy and deny that we have it; Americans speak of "democracy" as meaning political democracy and deny that they have it. Secretary Marshall said recently at Moscow that "To us a society is not free if law-abiding citizens live in fear of being denied the right to work or deprived of life, liberty, and the pursuit of happiness." The Soviet Encyclopedia of 1936 asserts that

"Democracy with capitalism is capitalistic democracy, a democracy of an exploiting minority directed against a majority—Soviet democracy does not exploit anybody—but with its dictatorship suppresses the exploiters smashed by the proletarian revolution—democracy is purely a class conception."

We resent and oppose any attempt by the Soviet Union to impose their concept of democracy upon us or to instil it into our midst by undercover propaganda. We cannot deny their right to resent and oppose any attempt of ours to impose or to instil our concept of democracy upon them. The fact that we have a conviction of the rightness of our view does not change this conclusion. They have a similar and probably more fanatical conviction of their "rightness." At an earlier day the term "legitimate" governments included, in the parlance of many in the western world, only those which were monarchical. Republican forms of government were acknowledged by the monarchs to be governments *de facto* but not *de jure*. Neither democracy nor Christianity can be imposed by the sword. The Christian missionary has supplanted the Crusader and the Spanish Inquisition. The missionary of our democracy is the demonstration of its success, its effectiveness, through every farm, factory, village, and city of these United States.

The international problem is not one of securing throughout the world an ideological uniformity which has never existed. No doubt Lincoln was correct in saying that the American Union could not continue to exist half slave and half free. But it has existed and can exist half Democratic and half Republican; half New Deal and half anti-New Deal. The world com-

munity has in the past existed half monarchical and
half republican; half Christian and half non-Christian.
In this series of lectures under the auspices of the
Associated Colleges at Claremont last year, Professor
Harold H. Fisher demonstrated most effectively that
the Soviet and American forms of government can
coexist in the world.

The Lincolnian precept can not be pressed in its
international application. The American Union, even
in the 1850's and 1860's, was a relatively homogeneous
unit. The world never has been and is not now such a
unit. The problem of international politics, vastly
more difficult than the American problem, is to find
the ways in which so many different peoples with so
many different traditions, so many different religious
and political and economic convictions, can coexist
without war. It is not in the American tradition to insist upon political any more than on economic monopoly. It is the American tradition to foster a system
of free political competition under regulations which
protect the weak from falling victim to the conflict
among the strong. It is our task to see to it that American democracy, as recently defined by Marshall and
by David Lilienthal, shall be vital enough to succeed
in such competition. It is our task, within the system
of the United Nations, to see to it that the weak shall
be free to choose their own ways of life, be those ways
American, or Russian, or something different from
either.

It may be profitable to examine the ways in which
the international community during the past two centuries has dealt with the problem of civil wars and of
governments which have been disapproved. It is par-

ticularly important to scan these pages of history for their lessons in view of the statement by President Truman in his historic speech to Congress on March 12. The President said: "I believe that it must be the policy of the United States to support free peoples who are resisting attempted subjugation by armed minorities or by outside pressures." Does this mean that we shall adopt the policy of saying, in a paraphrase of the words of our Constitution, that "The United States shall guarantee to every State in this World a Republican Form of Government, and shall protect each of them against invasion?" Is such a guarantee to be given by the United States alone or by the United Nations?

In recent times one of the most striking examples of the way in which a civil war may involve the peace of the world, is to be found in the Spanish Civil War of the 1930's. But Spain itself had afforded numerous earlier examples of the same fact. In 1698 the question was not one of Fascist or democratic control but of whether there should be Hapsburg or Bourbon domination of Europe. The great powers of Europe lined up on the two sides of the controversy. This developed into the War of the Spanish Succession in 1702 and by 1720 England had become the mistress of Gibraltar. When in 1808 Napoleon sought to put his brother Joseph on the Spanish throne, England rallied to the support of the other side. The establishment of a liberal government in 1820 in Spain led to two years of civil war and at the Congress of Verona in 1822 the powers decided to intervene, demanding the abrogation of the liberal constitution of 1812. This was the period when the Holy Alliance was campaigning against the extension of republicanism. Ten years

later in the Carlist revolt the powers were again lined
up in support of two opposing factions in Spain. Again
in 1869 the question of the succession to the Spanish
throne was part of the prelude to the outbreak of the
Franco-Prussian war.

The interest of the great powers in the domestic governmental affairs of other states in Europe was also displayed over and over again in the treatment of Balkan
affairs and of the fate of the Ottoman Empire. In 1878
the great powers said in regard to Serbia that, in claim-
ing "to enter the European family on the same basis as
other states" she "must previously recognize the principles which are the basis of social organization in all
States of Europe and accept them as a necessary condition of the favour which she asks for." In the Treaty
of Paris of 1856 the powers had agreed to respect the
independence and territorial integrity of the Ottoman
Empire and declared that they would consider any act
tending to violate this engagement as a question of
general interest.

In the western hemisphere, from the time of the
Spanish colonies' wars of liberation up through the
period of United States' hegemony, the United States
took an active interest in the form of government
which Latin American states adopted. Monroe's fa-
mous pronouncement included the proposition that we
would defend the republican form of government in
these countries against any attempt to reimpose upon
them the monarchical systems of Europe. Especially
in the latter part of the 19th century and in the first
years of this century, there were numerous instances
in which the action of this country determined what
individual or what group would rule in one of our

smaller neighbors to the south. Our action was by no means confined to instances in which there was a threat of foreign domination; frequently it was a question of a choice between two factions which were inspired by nothing more profound than the desire of individual leaders for wealth and power.

In 1907 the Republics of Central America made an attempt to put their regional house in order by agreeing among themselves that they would not recognize any new government which came into power through a revolution or *coup d'etat*. The United States announced that it would adopt the same principle as the basis of its policy in that area. The trend at this period is strongly in the direction of the maintenance of domestic peace and insistence that changes of government should not take place by other than orderly constitutional procedures. This trend finds its consolidation in the signature at Havana in 1928 of the Convention on Rights and Duties of States in Case of Civil Strife. This treaty, to which the United States and fourteen other American republics are parties, contains an agreement to prevent revolutionary movements from being organized or operating from the territory of any one of the signatory states. It includes an agreement to embargo shipment of arms to rebels, while permitting the shipments to the established governments.

Although this Havana Convention antedates the Good Neighbor Policy, it indicated another and most desirable trend toward collective action in the Western Hemisphere in cases of this kind. Thus, as one comes down to the current case of dissatisfaction with the government of Argentina, one finds the United States attempting to operate in conjunction with all of the other Latin American republics. Our failure to align all of the other republics with our policy is responsible for the present impasse. That failure, in turn, is at least partly due to Latin American dislike and fear of North American interferences in their civil strifes.

Turning to the Far East, one finds throughout the modern history of China examples of the joint concern of the great European powers and of the United States in the maintenance or in the creation of stable government. This policy was inspired less by a devotion to any great principle of democracy, than to the fear that some one power would take advantage of chaotic domestic conditions in China to establish a dominant position to the detriment of the other interested states. There was a formalization of this policy in the Washington Nine-Power Treaty of 1922, whereby the leading western countries and Japan agreed "to respect the sovereignty, the independence, and the territorial and administrative integrity of China." They agreed also "to provide the fullest and most unembarrassed opportunity to China to develop and maintain for herself an effective and stable government."

Although China emerged from World War II as one of the five great powers with permanent seats on the Security Council of the United Nations, the domestic difficulties in that country have not yet ceased. The United States through General Marshall sought to assist in bringing the contending factions together, but Marshall's statement of January 7, 1947, registered the failure of that effort. In that statement, the present Secretary of State frankly commented upon the difficulty of bringing together what he called "a dominant group of reactionaries" in the Kuomintang and the equally extreme members of the Chinese Communist party. He noted the existence of patriotic liberal elements in both groups, but his report marked the end of a policy of outright support for the established government. In the present Moscow Conference the affairs of China are obviously of concern to the "Big Three" but the United States declines to discuss them formally in China's absence.

In an earlier period, the interests of the United States and of Europe met in the Far East. With the realization of our world-wide interests and responsibilities which the Second World War brought about, joint American and European concern with the nature of the Spanish government appears. The United States has joined with the other members of the United Nations in condemning the Franco government and in applying certain pressures to bring about a change in that government. The contrast between our present attitude towards Spain and our attitude during the Spanish Civil War of the 1930's, is a striking indication of the development of world policy. Ten years ago the United States was not prepared to take an active part in the combined "non-intervention" measures agreed upon by the principal European states. But the Non-Intervention Agreement of the 1930's was inevitably itself an interference in the Spanish Civil War and its history was marked by flagrant intervention on the part of the Fascist states.

In the Yalta agreements we registered our concern in the establishment of representative governments in such countries as Poland and Bulgaria. We have been attempting, without much success, to ensure free elections of representative governments in those countries.

In Greece we participated by supplying 692 Americans to act as supervisors of the elections and we are now embarked upon a policy of throwing our full weight behind the government which was elected.

International law and practice have taken account of such situations as those which I have briefly sketched. The principle has been accepted that a state may lend support to an established government which is beset by insurrection without such action constituting intervention in the internal affairs of the country concerned. Aid to the insurrectionists, however, was considered to be intervention. This is the situation which a United States Federal Court had in mind in 1885 in saying "international law has no place for rebellion."[3] This was also the point of view which inspired the Mexican delegate in the League of Nations in 1937 when he made the following declaration concerning the Spanish Civil War: "The clear distinction made between a government victim of aggression to whom every material and moral assistance should be afforded, and aggressor groups who should certainly not be granted facilities enabling them to continue the struggle with greater bloodshed, should be extended to cases of military rebellion such as that which has occurred in Spain."[4] The difficulty with this point of view is that while it was applicable to the Mexican government's sympathy with the established Spanish government in 1937, it is not applicable to the Mexican government's disapproval of the Franco government in 1947.

The principle justifying support of established gov-

---

[3] The Ambrose Light, 25 F. 408 (1885).
[4] League of Nations, *Official Journal,* March-April 1937, p. 264.

ernments was frequently utilized by the United States in cases of revolutions in Latin America. Under the authority of joint resolutions passed by Congress in 1912 and 1922, the President could impose arms embargoes covering shipments to rebellious factions in Latin American countries. But the President was not required to impose such embargoes and when the United States favored a rebellious faction, the refusal to impose an arms embargo could work to the advantage of the insurrectionists.

When a civil war attained such proportions as to involve two organized groups, each purporting to exercise governmental authority and contending through well-organized forces, it became the regular international practice for other states to recognize the belligerency of the two parties. Once belligerency was recognized, the outside states became subject to the obligations of the law of neutrality. This meant that the two factions were to be treated on equal terms just as in the case of a war between two sovereign states. Such was the position of Great Britain and other powers during our own Civil War and the principle was recognized in the Havana Treaty of 1928 which has already been described.

One of the troubles with the application of the neutrality system was that legal impartiality frequently represented factual partiality. Thus in the Italo-Ethiopian War the United States was scrupulously correct in forbidding American nationals to take passage on either Italian or Ethiopian trans-Atlantic liners. In many other instances the equality of treatment which neutrality required would work to the advantage of one or the other party to the civil war depending upon which one had control of the ports and thus could take advantage of impartial commerce with the rest of the world.

The League of Nations Covenant contained no specific provisions concerning civil wars and the League's system broke down when it tried to grapple with the Spanish Civil War. The League Covenant did contain in Article 10 a provision similar to part of Section 4 of Article IV of the United States Constitution, in declaring that the members of the League would guarantee their fellow members against external aggressions; there was not, however, any guarantee of the maintenance of a "republican form of government" in each member state.

In the United Nations Charter the problem of protection against external aggression is not covered by any specific provision comparable to that in Article 10 of the Covenant of the League. It was felt that the general provisions of the Charter relative to the preservation of international peace sufficed for this purpose. Again, however, nothing specific was provided to cover the cases of civil wars. Paragraph 7 of Article 2 of the Charter might seem to look in the other direction since it provides that nothing in the Charter "shall authorize the United Nations to intervene in matters which are essentially within the domestic jurisdiction of any state." The definition of domestic questions presents numerous difficulties. As the Spanish and French delegates to the League of Nations pointed out in 1936, it is "increasingly difficult to draw a dividing line between the internal and the international aspects of a nation's life."⁵ Who would assert that the problem of domestic governments in Greece or in China or in Spain or in Bulgaria or in the Argentine, is .today a question devoid of international implications? The question whether action will be taken in any particular case depends upon the surrounding political circumstances. The United Nations has taken action in regard to the Franco government in Spain where civil war is not flagrant now. At this moment no one is taking definite official action in regard to the actual civil war in China. The United States, acting inside or outside the machinery of the United Nations, is avowedly ready to take action in Greece, and the Soviet government, without an equally frank declaration, concerns itself with the establishment of "friendly governments" in countries adjacent to its borders.

The United Nations, so far as the general framework of its Charter is concerned, could take action in regard to a situation such as that in Greece. The historical record amply demonstrates that a condition of internal disturbance in any state may constitute a threat to the peace of the world at large. The Security Council, therefore, would be competent to take action under the Charter in cases of civil strife. Such action by the Security Council, however, may be blocked by an exercise of the veto power. But history also indicates that effective action can be taken without the direct kind of intervention which the Security Council might authorize under Chapter VII of the Charter. For example, financial assistance and provision for ex-

---

⁵ Hans Wehberg, *Civil War and International Law,* (Trans. by J. L. Mowat,) extract from *The World Crisis,* a symposium, Longmans Green & Co., 1938, p. 187.

pert technicians could be agreed to by the United Nations through a vote to which the veto power would not extend. The United Nations Food and Agriculture Organization issued on March 16 a report of a study made in Greece last summer by a commission of eleven members, of whom six were Americans, including the chairman, President Franklin S. Harris of Utah Agricultural College. This international commission analyzed some of the economic ills to which President Truman later referred in his message. It recommended that assistance be provided under United Nations auspices. It recommended an initial loan of $100,000,000 by the International Bank for Reconstruction and Development. Technical assistance could be provided through agencies functioning under the Economic and Social Council. A European economic commission designed to assist in European economic reconstruction and recovery has already been endorsed by the General Assembly.

The New York Times has pointed out editorially that this mission of the Food and Agricultural Organization was international and non-political, yet "had the courage to speak out for democracy." It may be added that while the International Bank would properly hesitate to float a loan which would be a bad financial risk, the League of Nations found ways to finance Austria and five other countries after World War I under a system of international guarantees. United States' participation in a guarantee of an international loan to Greece could not be more expensive than direct unilateral loans or gifts to the same country. It is said that the United Nations has no funds to help Greece directly; neither has President Truman. Congress could appropriate money for international as well as for unilateral aid. Appropriate supervision and safeguards for the expenditure of the funds could be devised. It would be quite in accord with international precedent to accept a formula which determined the quotas of supervisory personnel in proportion to national financial contributions, direct or by guaranty.

It is said that the United Nations cannot act quickly; it has not been demonstrated that in such a matter it cannot act as quickly as the Congress of the United States.

With reference to the security aspects of the situation, Walter Lippman has pointed out that under Article 106 of the Charter we are obliged to consult with Great Britain and the Soviet Union and France and with other members of the United Nations, on questions involving the maintenance of international peace and security during this transitional period before the Security Council is equipped to act.

A special meeting of the General Assembly, which reaches its decisions by majority vote, could be convened. Such a special session is projected to deal with the Palestinian situation; it could deal with the Greek and Turkish situations also. It is true that under Article 12 of the Charter, the General Assembly cannot make a recommendation in regard to a situation which is being considered by the Security Council, but only a part of the Greek situation is before the Council. Under Article 66 of the Charter, the Economic and Social Council—which also acts by majority vote—could be authorized by the General Assembly to supervise the economic reconstruction of Greece. It is probably true that no organ of the United Nations could properly undertake to train or equip either the Greek or the Turkish army. If such action seems to the United States to be necessary "for the purpose of maintaining international peace and security" we should consult with other states as required by Article 106. Such consultations would probably not result in unanimous agreement but the United States might thereafter, without doing violence to the Charter, enter into bilateral agreements with the Greek and Turkish governments for military training missions and for loans, as we have done with various Latin American governments. Since I do not pretend to be a Russian expert I shall not hazard guesses whether such bilateral agreements would promote our essential basic policy of finding a way to get on with the Soviet government. I do not challenge the President's sincerity in believing that his policy of strengthening the Greek and Turkish governments will promote peace. I do challenge the wisdom of the method which he originally proposed and which has already had two very bad effects in spite of later clarifications by Senator Austin before the Security Council:

First—It has stimulated and encouraged those in this country who argue that we must fight the U.S.S.R. some day and that we had better do it now while we have a monopoly of atomic bombs even though this would be a blatant violation of our pledged word;

Second—It has weakened the United Nations at a time when all our effort should be devoted to strengthening it.

Senator Austin's speech in the Security Council on March 28 was evidently designed to repair some of the damage caused by the phrasing of President Truman's

A similar ineptness in American diplomacy was apparent at the San Francisco Conference when the United States delegation allowed itself to get into the position of opposing Soviet proposals for inserting in the Charter provisions regarding the equality of women. This was a relatively slight matter, but there was another instance of graver importance when a similar alignment appeared regarding the question of mentioning the word "independence" as an ultimate objective of dependent peoples. That same theme has again arisen in the debates at Lake Success concerning the American proposals for a trusteeship of the Japanese-mandated islands. Again the Soviet Union appeared to be the champion of dependent peoples by insisting on the inclusion of a similar reference to eventual independence. The United States eventually acquiesced; it should have been out in front if it wished to maintain a moral as well as a material leadership.

In undertaking now to throw the weight of the United States behind the principle of self-determination for the peoples of the small states of Europe, it will be perhaps some day necessary to declare frankly whether we will permit such states to choose a communist form of government if we are assured that such a form of government expresses the free will of the people and is not imposed upon them by outside pressure. Senator Austin told the Security Council that we would do so. It will always be necessary to bear in mind the wise precept framed by Elihu Root in drafting the instructions to the commission which went out to the Philippines when we assumed the government of those islands. The commission was told that they "should bear in mind that the government which they are establishing is designed, not for our satisfaction or for the expression of our theoretical views, but for the happiness, peace, and prosperity of the Philippine islands, and the measures adopted should be made to conform to their customs, their habits, and even their prejudices, to the fullest extent consistent with the accomplishment of the indispensable requisites of just and effective government."[7]

No community or social group is free from disagreements and quarrels. This is true whether the group is the family, a fraternal order, capital and labor, the City of Los Angeles, the State of California, the United States, the United Nations, or the world. The problem is always the problem of striking a balance. Especially in politics there is always danger in assuming at any moment that there is an absolute right or wrong. Political concepts change with the times. What was right to the American colonists was wrong to the Tories. What was right to the Old Guard in the Republican Party thirty-five years ago was wrong to the Progressives. What was right to the New Deal was wrong to the Republicans. Each group must have the courage of its convictions, but the objective of civilization is to adjust conflicts without resort to force. I believe personally that our system of government is infinitely better than the Russian. I do not believe that our concept, or theirs, can successfully be imposed by force of arms. I regard the imposition of any way of life upon a people by the armed force and terrorism of a police state like the Soviet Union, as being just as abhorrent as imposition by an invading

---

[7] Jessup, Elihu Root, (1938) Vol. I, p. 356.

army. What single state can be both all-wise and all-powerful and, as it surveys the world, undertake to determine who shall govern in each of the countries of the world? Are we or is the U.S.S.R. or is Argentina to decide whether the established government or the revolutionists more nearly represent today the best interests of the people of Paraguay? When Great Britain has finally abandoned its imperial right to judge in India, is any single other state to assert the right to intervene on behalf of either Hindus or Moslems if those two groups are still unable to reach amicable agreement? Surely there is no hope of progress in the unilateral ways of diplomacy.

The new responsibilities of the United States have properly brought us to the abandonment of an isolationism which would pretend that the affairs of lands once considered distant, are of no interest or concern to us. Our new position of world primacy has also led us to accept the United Nations as the key to our foreign policy. A foreign policy based on the United Nations is a policy of multilateral decision and action, not a policy of unilateral decision and action.

Assume for a moment that the United Nations could reach a unanimous decision regarding the desirability of a change in some domestic governmental situation. So far as the states possessing the veto power are concerned, such unanimity was achieved in the disapproval of the Franco government in Spain despite the fact that in this western part of the Mediterranean as in the eastern part, conflict between British and other national political interests was apparent two centuries before the advent of communism as a world force. In the case of Spain today, United Nations pressure is confined to the withdrawal of ambassadors and exclusions from participation in various international organizations. Suppose it were decided to go further, what could the United Nations do?

The horribly simple method of dropping a few atomic bombs from planes displaying an international symbol of their mission, is impossible. The police or the F.B.I. do not dynamite or burn down a whole city block full of men, women, and children, in order to get rid of a group of gangsters known to be hiding there.

Similarly economic pressure in the form of an international blockade, starves the innocent before the guilty since the latter have the power and will utilize the last supplies of food, fuel, and clothing to support their own adherents.

There is the possibility of the use of international police forces sufficiently strong to overpower local resistance without prolonged devastating warfare. Winston Churchill in the House of Commons proposed such a plan for Spain in 1937. It might be contemplated in any such plan that the international forces would administer the country, as Germany and Japan are now administered, until the people could freely elect a government of their own choosing. When international organization is perfected, this system may prevail.

There is also the policy of maintaining the established government despite its defects. This is the general theory which international law has sanctioned, which is embodied in the Inter-American Convention concluded at Havana in 1928 and which seems to underlie our policy in Greece today. It is also subject to the stresses and strains implicit in foreign sympathies for or against this or that faction. Pushed to its logical extremes it might result in an international treaty making rebellion against any established government an international crime. Something of the sort was attempted in 1937 when as a result of the assassination of King Alexander of Yugoslavia in Marseilles, there was drafted under League of Nations auspices an abortive treaty for the suppression of terrorism and terroristic crime. But recall the fact that in 1851 when Louis Kossuth sought to free Hungary from Austrian rule, he was hailed in the United States, not as a criminal, but as the nation's guest, feted and honored by private persons and groups from New York to the Mississippi. He was formally received by both Houses of Congress and dined with the President. To the Austrian protest, Secretary of State Daniel Webster replied that the American people had the right "to sympathize with the efforts of any nation to acquire liberty." But imperial Austria suppressed the Hungarian revolution with the aid of Russian troops.

Rigorous non-intervention, allowing the country to work out its own salvation or to "stew in its own juice," is somewhat less objectionable on humanitarian grounds. Its effectiveness can be increased by international border or sea and air patrols to check evasion of the international boycott. But the unhappy experience with the Spanish Non-Intervention Agreement of 1936 is not encouraging. Those in other countries who sympathize passionately with one side or the other will object violently, particularly as this or that group seems to be attaining supremacy. Simultaneously, however, there can be continuous diplomatic

pressure to induce acceptance of international supervision of free elections. If that pressure is loyally unanimous, it may succeed, depending on the country concerned. It might succeed in Greece or in Paraguay or
in Spain. It probably would not succeed in India or in
China (leaving aside the fact that China as the holder
of a veto-right in the Security Council could prevent
the attainment of the necessary unanimity). It probably could not even be tried out where the established
government, as in Poland, has the strong backing of a
veto-wielding member of the Security Council.

A fundamental question is: Shall the preservation of
the world's peace be exalted over the attainment of a
"republican form of government" in every country of
the world? I would answer "Yes." Some people be-
moan what they consider to be the fact that in this
country many persons are more concerned about personal security than about individual liberty. It is said
that liberty is being sacrificed on the altar of state
paternalism which promises security. It is argued that
this is a sign of softness, of a weakening of our native
lust for freedom. I shall not divert from my main
theme to debate this domestic question. From the
international standpoint, I affirm that if we allow a civil
strife to broaden and degenerate into a general international war between the advocates of two opposing
factions, representing two opposing theories of government, we settle nothing. War breeds its own flock
of troubles, ideologies, demagogues, and further wars.

Nevertheless there is great danger in sweeping
generalizations. As already suggested, a solution suitable to the situation in one country is not suitable to
that in another. There are occasions where society

must insist upon the resignation of the use of violence. We have adopted that principle in our own American society with reference to insurrection; we are struggling to make that principle generally applicable to strife between management and labor. That principle can operate only if there are procedures for peaceful adjustment. In the domestic labor field we are slow in finding these procedures. In the international field inevitably we move on still more leaden feet.

The world will not overnight be composed of model governments, partly because it is not yet even composed of groups of people competent to operate republican forms of government. Many peoples must still pass through generations of tutelage. Some of their masters will be benevolent; some will be malevolent. Some will seek to lead and to educate by disinterested progressive methods which you and I like to think are characteristic of the United States. Some will seek to instill wisdom with the birch rod or its political equivalents, the concentration camp and the machine gun.

The classic appeal, "Come over into Macedonia and help us," has a new meaning today. Our ears will never be deaf to such appeals. They were not deaf when the natives in the Congo were abused some forty years ago. They were not deaf when the Turks massacred the Christians in Armenia, when Czarist Russia persecuted the Jews, when the Nazis embarked on their career of genocide.

But let us keep our emotions straight even while we keep our powder dry. In the present Greek situation there are at least three interwoven factors which were not sharply distinguished in President Truman's speech. In setting forth those three factors by way of conclusion I recognize the risk of over-simplification and that I do not venture to suggest detailed solutions of all our problems. But it is in the light of the immediate issue in Greece that we may test the long range policy of international guaranty of democratic government.

First. There is the problem of economic reconstruction in Greece. Here the international commission of the Food and Agriculture Organization has clearly pointed the way to international action under the United Nations. To such international action we are committed and in it lies the only hope of future world peace and progress.

Second. There is the problem of communism. This too is not essentially a new problem although the labels are new. We see in communism a threat to our established institutions, economic, social, and political. Monarchial Europe saw the same threat in the republicanism of revolutionary France. That Europe of one hundred and fifty years ago shuddered also at the excesses of the French Terror as abolitionists shuddered at the cruelty of the slavocracy and as we are aroused and appalled by the cruelty of the police state. Slavery was ended indeed by our Civil War with its sad aftermath of the carpet-bag governments and a long heritage of bitterness. Our ultimate success ensued despite our failure to find the right process for attaining the objective. It is a commonplace assertion that communism, or any other revolutionary creed, finds most fertile soil where there is already autocratic government and economic distress. The victory of our concept of democracy lies in its own demonstration of its values and its effectiveness and in its ability from its strength

and self-restraint to persuade and help—not force—
other peoples to choose our road.

Third. There is the problem of power politics—the
expansion of Russia. This is not a new problem. It
dominated much of the international politics of the
nineteenth century. Russia cast envious eyes on the
Turkish Straits long before the dawn of communism.
Russia and England clashed and defined their spheres
of influence in Persia long before there was a United
Nations Security Council to discuss the Iranian complaint of Russian influence in Azerbaidjan. In this
sense we are indeed the inheritors of century-old British policy. It is precisely the reverse of Kipling's line
that "there is neither East nor West—when two strong
men meet face to face." The history of modern Europe teaches the failure of the system of balance of
power to solve the perennial conflict of two strong
vital nations or groups of nations. I, for one, reject
absolutely the idea of an "American Century" in
which the United States in complacent benevolence
will tell the rest of the world and each part of it what
is good for it. There remains the experiment of international cooperation, briefly and unsuccessfully tried
by the League of Nations between the two wars.
"With firmness in the right" that is a road which we
can travel, not with blind optimism and not with
utter confidence, but with hope.

Professor Fisher, in the lectures which I have already mentioned, stated eloquently the view which
Mr. Eric Johnston of the United States Chamber of
Commerce also expounded. In Professor Fisher's
words:

"The paramount issue of our time is whether in the

world community now taking shape, these two un-
conquerable powers shall work together in leadership
in the unity of that community, or whether each, sus-
picious and fearful of the other, gathers allies about
itself and stores up more terrible engines of destruction
to get ready for a conflict which will prove with awful
finality man's incapacity to save himself from the mis-
use of the knowledge and skill he has acquired."[8]

---

[8] Harold H. Fisher, *America and Russia in the World Community*,
(1946) p. 7.